HEAVENLY BODIES

Earth is one of nine planets in the solar system. One Moon orbits our planet. Earth can be explored from space like any other heavenly body. Studying the earth as an astronomical body must be done from a satellite or spacecraft. This view of Earth has been taken far enough away to show the Moon and stars.

AN ANCIENT CALENDAR

In ancient Egypt, the year was divided into 36 weeks of 10 days each. Each week started when a particular star group, called a decan, rose in the sky. This ceiling (left) from the temple at Dendera shows a circle supported by goddesses. Round the outside ring are figures representing the decans. In the centre of the circle are the signs of the zodiac. The gods, holding wands, represent planets.

SPACE
-A TIME LINE-

~c.3000 BC~

Egyptians use stars to mark the weeks in their calendar

~c.300~

Aristarchus teaches that Earth circles the Sun

~c.100~

Hipparchus compiles a catalogue of stars. He constructs a model of the Sun circling the Earth: to allow for seasons Earth is slightly off-centre in the circle.

~c. AD 150~

Ptolemy publishes several books on astronomy, including the Almagest. He makes a list of 1080 stars, divided into 48 constellations, and tables from which the movements of the Sun, Moon and planets can be worked out. He teaches that the Earth is the centre of the universe.

~c.1150~

Chinese invent rockets

BARON MUNCHAUSEN

People have dreamed of travelling in space for centuries, though it is only in the latter half of the 20th century that they have achieved it. Baron Munchausen, the hero of an amazing collection of tall stories published by Rudolf Erich Raspe in 1785, disdained any form of spacecraft - he used a fast-growing bean to reach the Moon!

PTOLEMY

Ptolemy, or Claudius Ptolemaeus (AD 90-168) lived in Alexandria in Egypt. He was an astronomer and geographer who listed 48 constellations, or groups of stars, giving their positions in the heavens. Ptolemy argued that the Earth was a sphere and believed the Moon, Sun, planets and stars moved round the Earth at different speeds. Many of his ideas were taken from an earlier Greek astronomer, Hipparchus. Ptolemy published his ideas in a book known as *Almagest*, which translated means 'the greatest'.

Exploring by Eye

The earliest astronomers were not interested in how the universe worked. They needed to know when to plant or harvest crops, when rivers would flood, or when there would be an eclipse. They used the movements of bodies in the heavens to make calendars, and to predict events in the future. Consequently they became astrologers, as well as astronomers. It was the ancient Greeks who first started to ask questions about the universe and how it worked. They were interested in the movements of the planets, the wandering bodies they could see in the night sky. They wanted to prove that the movement of planets was regular, and could be accurately predicted. To try and do this, they used geometry.

COPERNICUS

Nicolaus Copernicus (1473-1543) is the father of modern astronomy. From his studies he saw that some of Ptolemy's ideas did not work. Ptolemy implied that the Moon's size changed, but it obviously did not. In the *Almagest*, Ptolemy looked at each planet separately, and it was clear that they were in some way connected. Aristarchus (c.310-230 BC) thought that Earth and the other planets revolved around the Sun. Copernicus thought this was the simplest and most systematic reason for the movement of heavenly bodies. He could not prove this Sun-centred (heliocentric) theory, but it made much more sense than the Earth-centred (geocentric) explanations.

EXPLORATION
of
SPACE

BY

FELICITY TROTMAN

What is Space?

Space is the name for the part of the universe between heavenly bodies like galaxies, stars and planets. It is not empty. There are such things as clouds of dust and gas in space. Exploring space and all it contains is the greatest challenge facing mankind.

In space, distances are measured in light years. This is the distance travelled by light in one year – 946,000,000,000,000 kilometres (588,000,000,000,000 miles). In thousands of years we have only just begun to explore Space. As the third millennium begins a new generation – you – will take up the challenge.

DUSTY PATCHES

This cloudy patch is called a nebula. Some nebulae are galaxies, made up of thousands of millions of stars and many light-years away. Others are patches of dust and gas in our own Galaxy, the Milky Way.

FALLING SKIES

Space is full of dust and pieces of rock. When they enter Earth's atmosphere, most of them burn up and we see meteors, or shooting stars. Sometimes a larger piece of rock reaches the surface of Earth before it burns up and hits the ground as a meteorite. For thousands of years meteorites were the only objects from space that could be studied. This woodcut made in 1508 shows a meteorite splitting a tree in half.

CLOCKWORK MODELS

Astronomers have been exploring the solar system, the planets and other objects that orbit the star we call our Sun, for thousands of years. An orrery is a clockwork model of the solar system in which the planets orbit the sun in the centre.

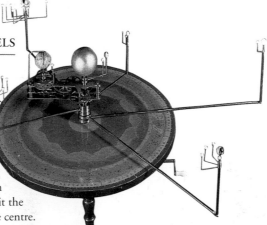

SKY WATCHING

The skies have been watched from earliest times. Observatories are buildings from which astronomers study the skies. This one, El Caracol, was built by the Mayan astronomers of Chichen Itza, in what is now Mexico.

CENTRE OF THE UNIVERSE?

Early astronomers thought that the Earth was the centre of the heavens. They believed that Earth was fixed, and that the Sun, Moon and planets circled round it. They thought each planet (the Sun and Moon counted as planets) was carried by a transparent sphere of crystal that moved. Above and beyond the planets was a sphere to which the stars were fixed. This diagram (left) shows this geocentric system.

TEACHING TOOLS

An armillary sphere is a 3D diagram of the heavens. The circles stand for the celestial equator, the zodiac, and other circles in the sky. Armillary spheres were used for teaching, and for taking measurements.

SET IN STONE

Around 1000 BC the people of Mesopotamia were interested in the heavens. This boundary stone shows the Sun, the Moon, Venus, and zodiac signs. The zodiac is the group of 12 constellations the Sun and the planets seem to travel past during the year. They were thought to be important in predicting the future.

SUN-CENTRED

This diagram (above) shows Copernicus's heliocentric theory of the universe. The Sun is at the centre, with the six known planets revolving in circles around it. Copernicus published his ideas in a book, *De Revolutionibus Orbium Coelestium*, just before he died in 1543.

NEW MOONS

Muslim astronomers were particularly interested in the Moon. The Muslim month starts when the new Moon is first seen, so it was extremely important to know when this was going to happen. Muslims pray at least five times a day, so astronomers also needed to work out exactly when sunset, nightfall, daybreak, midday and afternoon were going to be. Many mosques employed astronomers as timekeepers. This picture shows astronomers in Istanbul around 1577. There are books on shelves, and many instruments, including quadrants, a compass and an armillary sphere. There is a clock on the table and a globe at the bottom.

Exploring Space with Telescopes

England was a maritime nation, and sailors used stars for navigation. King Charles II founded the Royal Observatory at Greenwich in 1675. Astronomers were asked to try and find a good way of working out the longitude of a place.

Galileo was the first person to look at the night sky with a telescope, and in doing so he revolutionized the study of the heavens. Telescopes quickly disproved the old idea of crystal spheres around Earth, and revealed a whole universe that waited to be explored. Galileo himself made some important discoveries, including four moons orbiting Jupiter, Saturn's rings, craters on the Moon, individual stars in the Milky Way, and sunspots, from which he worked out that the Sun itself rotated. Refracting telescopes, like Galileo's, and the new reflecting telescopes showed far more detail than naked eye observation. Bigger telescopes, with better lenses, enabled astronomers to make more and more discoveries.

HERSCHEL'S 40-FOOT TELESCOPE

On 13th March 1781, Sir William Herschel (1738-1822) discovered the planet Uranus, using a 7-foot home-made reflecting telescope. The biggest telescope he built was this 40-foot reflector, but it was awkward to use. The mirror had been made with extra copper, and tarnished easily.

GALILEO'S TELESCOPES

Galileo's most powerful telescope could enlarge an image up to 30 times. This is about the same magnification as a pair of modern binoculars. These telescopes are refracting telescopes, that is they have lenses at each end of a tube, giving the best magnification.

GALILEO'S BELIEFS

Galileo Galilei (1564-1642) was an Italian mathematician, physicist and astronomer who came into conflict with the Roman Catholic church because he supported Copernicus's heliocentric theory. He was forbidden to teach the new ideas, and then, when it became clear that he had not changed his mind, he was tried by the Inquisition. Threatened with torture, he publicly recanted, though privately he still believed Copernicus.

NEWTON'S TELESCOPE

Sir Isaac Newton (1642-1727) was an English physicist and mathematician known for working out the law of gravitation. He also designed an easy-to-use reflecting telescope in 1668. A reflecting telescope uses a shaped mirror to reflect and magnify images.

SPACE
-A Time Line-

~1543~
Copernicus publishes De revolutionibus. *He states that Earth circles the Sun.*

~1575 - 80~
Istanbul Observatory built

~1610~
Galileo looks at the sky through a telescope

~1668~
Isaac Newton builds his reflecting telescope

~1675~
Greenwich Observatory founded

~1781~
William Herschel discovers the planet Uranus

~1845~
Lord Rosse, using the 'Leviathan of Parsonstown' telescope, finds that nebulae have a spiral shape

~1846~
J G Galle in Berlin finds the planet Neptune, as predicted by John Couch Adams in England and Urbain Le Verrier in France

SPIRALLING NEBULAE

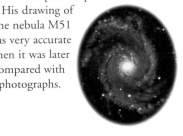

To study nebulae, the Earl of Rosse built a gigantic reflecting telescope in the grounds of his castle at Parsonstown in Ireland. In 1845, Rosse discovered that some nebulae were a spiral shape. His drawing of the nebula M51 was very accurate when it was later compared with photographs.

SISTERLY LOVE

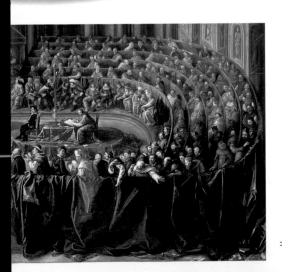

In 1772, Herschel brought his sister Caroline from Hanover to England to help him. When she was not acting as her brother's secretary and assistant, Caroline watched the sky with her own telescope, looking for comets. By 1797, she had found eight.

CABBAGE PATCH ROCKETS

American Robert Goddard (1882-1945) made practical experiments with rockets and different fuels. On 16 March, 1926, he launched the first rocket to use a liquid propellant – from his Aunt Effie's cabbage patch!

FROM FICTION TO FACT

Early rocket pioneers were inspired by two adventure stories by Frenchman Jules Verne. In *De la Terre à la Lune* (1865) and *Autour de la Lune* (1870), he describes the adventures of his three-man crew, launched into space by cannon. Now that men have been to the Moon, amazing similarities between the real moonshots and Verne's stories can be seen. For example, his launch took place in Florida near Cape Kennedy. This is near the equator, where the speed of Earth's rotation is greatest and helps a rocket escape Earth's gravity more easily. Verne's cannon was called the Columbiad. The command module of Apollo 11 was named Columbia. Verne even described a test flight using animals in a scaled-down model.

LAUNCH VEHICLES

Ariane is the rocket used as a launch vehicle by the European Space Agency, ESA. Many satellites, as well as the Giotto probe, have been launched by Ariane. When a rocket is fired, the burning propellants makes hot gases which expand, and escape from the base of the rocket. This force, called thrust, lifts the rocket off the ground.

WERNHER VON BRAUN

Wernher von Braun (1912-1977) was born in Germany. He helped to produce the V2 rocket, which was used as a weapon against Britain during World War II. Later, von Braun went to America where he helped on the space programme, including designing the Saturn V rocket.

OVERCOMING GRAVITY

Konstantin Tsiolkovsky (1857-1935) studied maths, physics and astronomy. Inspired by Jules Verne's space stories, Tsiolkovsky thought about how to overcome gravity and realised that rockets were the key to space flight. He worked out the basic theory of rocket propulsion, including using liquid propellants, and the amount of fuel a rocket would need to go into orbit.

Rockets

Exploring space from Earth is strictly limited. We could explore more if we got off Earth. There have been many writers who have imagined that it was possible to do this, but only in the last half of the twentieth century has any object been sent into space from Earth. To escape the gravitational pull of Earth, a vehicle has to travel at 40,200 kilometres an hour (about 25,000 miles per hour), or 11 kilometres a second (7 miles per second). The only engine that can produce this kind of energy is a rocket. Rockets were invented by the Chinese around 1150. These rockets burned gunpowder, and were used as weapons. Around 1500, the Chinese scientist Wan Hu tried to fly, using 47 rockets tied to his sedan chair. The rockets exploded, and Wan Hu was never seen again. It was only in 1903 that the Russian Konstantin Tsiolkovsky suggested using rockets to reach space.

JAPANESE HOPES

The Japanese NASDA (National Space Development Agency) has space centres at Kagoshima and Tanegashima. They hope to investigate the Sun, Moon and Mars using their two-stage HII rocket

MOON ROCKET

Saturn V, the rocket used to launch the manned Apollo spacecraft to the Moon, was the biggest rocket ever built. Saturn V was a three-stage rocket. The first stage was powerful enough to lift the rocket from the launch pad. When the fuel was used up, the first stage separated and fell back to Earth. The second stage then fired, and the lighter rocket travelled higher and faster. The third stage lifted the spacecraft into its flightpath.

Sputnik & Other Satellites

On 4 October 1957, the world was thrilled and excited to hear a beeping sound from space. The Soviet Union had launched Sputnik (it means 'traveller'), the first ever artificial satellite in space. In January 1958, America launched its first satellite, Explorer 1. This was the start of the Space Age. Since then, thousands of satellites have been launched for collecting scientific information, communication, navigation, spying, and weather forecasting, as well as astronomy. Some kinds of radiation, such as X-rays, infrared and ultraviolet, cannot penetrate the atmosphere, and cannot be studied from Earth. Astronomical satellites above Earth's atmosphere can work without interference.

POLLUTION CHECKS

The American space agency NASA (the National Aeronautics and Space Administration) planned a 'Mission to Planet Earth' programme of satellites. Responding to concerns about pollution, the first satellite in the series was the Upper Atmosphere Research Satellite, launched in 1991. It checks changes in the ozone layer.

SPUTNIK

Sputnik 1 was a steel sphere weighing 84 kilos (184 lbs), with a diameter of 58 centimetres (23 inches). Sputnik orbited the Earth once every 96 minutes, 17 seconds, travelling at heights varying from 228 kilometres (142 miles) to 947 kilometres (589 miles). It sent out radio signals for 21 days.

SMALL BUT POWERFUL

Explorer 1, America's first satellite, orbited Earth for 12 years collecting information on temperatures, meteorites and cosmic rays. It discovered the Van Allen radiation belt, 600 miles above Earth. Fifty-five Explorer scientific satellites were launched over a period of 30 years.

TELSTAR

Telstar I was the first communications satellite. Built in America by the Bell Telephone Company, it was launched in 1962. It used microwave radiation and solar power to relay telephone and radio signals. It also had a TV channel, which was used to make the first live broadcast from the USA to Europe.

SPACE RACERS!

Verney and Gordy, two rhesus monkeys, took part in research on blood flow in space. They were launched along with rats, newts, insects and plants in a joint Soviet-American biospace mission. They returned to Earth successfully a week later.

LOST IN SPACE

Sputnik 2 carried a dog called Laika into space. Tests showed that she had not been affected by the launch, or by being weightless. However, it was not possible to bring the satellite back and Laika died in space.

RATS

Strapped in for take-off! Hector the white rat's body systems were monitored by scientists during his flight in space. Many animals were sent into space to see what happened to them. Scientists needed as much information as they could get before they dared send a human into space.

SPACE
-A Time Line-

~1865, 1870~

Jules Verne publishes his two inspirational novels De la Terre à la Lune *(From the Earth to the Moon) and* Autour de la Lune *(Round the Moon)*

~1903~

Konstantin Tsiolkovsy publishes the theory of rocket propulsion in The Exploration of Cosmic Space by Means of Reaction Devices

~1919~

Robert Goddard publishes the results of his rocket experiments, including his belief that a rocket could reach the Moon, in A Method of Reaching Extreme Altitudes

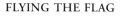

MISSION BADGE

The first men on the Moon wore this badge, designed by Michael Collins. It shows an American bald eagle landing on the Moon with an olive branch in its claws. The sunshine on Earth in the background is coming from the wrong direction – it should light the top, not the side.

FLYING THE FLAG

While Michael Collins flew the Command Module in orbit around the Moon, Edwin 'Buzz' Aldrin (left and above) and Neil Armstrong landed on the surface, in the Sea of Tranquility, on 20 July, 1969. The American flag is wired to hold it out as though the wind is blowing it.

EVERLASTING

There is no wind on the Moon, so Neil Armstrong's footprint - the first on the Moon - will last for ever.

FAR SIDE OF THE MOON

Until this picture was taken by Luna 3, humans had never seen the far side of the Moon. As it orbits Earth, the Moon rotates, keeping the same side facing us.

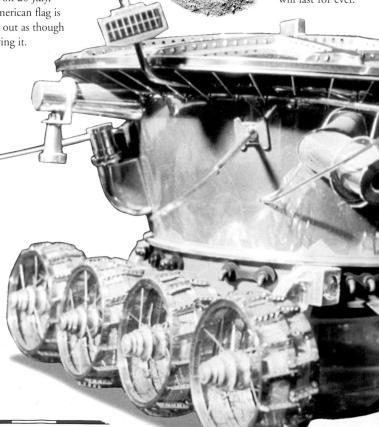

Moonshots

The Moon is our nearest neighbour in space, orbiting the planet at a distance of around 384,403 kilometres (221,456 miles). Only 12 men have ever walked on it. For mankind's first journey into space, the Moon was the obvious place to aim for. Soviet Luna probes were the first to reach the Moon. Luna 2 crash-landed on the Moon, and Luna 3 took the first photograph ever of the far side of the Moon. In May, 1961, American Alan Shepard went into space for 15 minutes. In a speech to congress, President Kennedy challenged the nation to put a man on the Moon before the end of the decade. America succeeded and made six moon landings.

THE RACE TO SPACE

The goal of putting a man on the Moon was a huge challenge to American scientists. Enthusiasm for the project was enormous, and the desire to beat the Soviet Union very strong. As a result, America put men on the Moon in less than 10 years. Apollo 11, carrying the first astronauts to land on the Moon, was launched on 16 July 1969.

LUNOKHOD

Lunokhod was a roving vehicle sent to the Moon in the unmanned Soviet probe Luna 17, launched in 1970. It was driven by remote control from Earth. Television cameras on the front allowed scientists to explore the Moon.

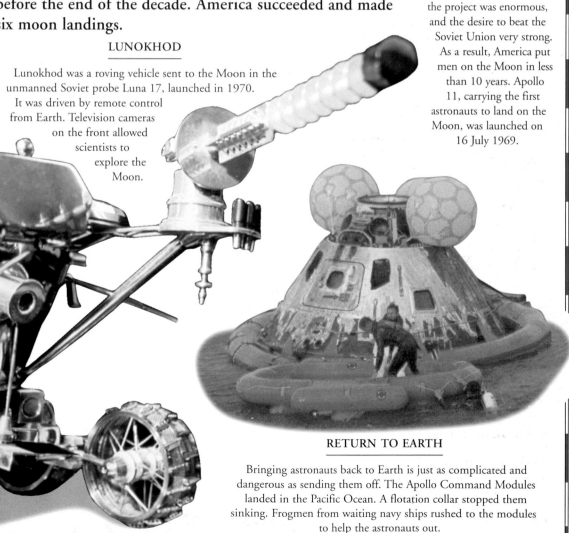

RETURN TO EARTH

Bringing astronauts back to Earth is just as complicated and dangerous as sending them off. The Apollo Command Modules landed in the Pacific Ocean. A flotation collar stopped them sinking. Frogmen from waiting navy ships rushed to the modules to help the astronauts out.

Astronauts

To fly a vehicle into space needs a highly trained group of men and women. Astronauts must be fit to cope with the physical demands of weightlessness, and they also have to be able to understand the technical complexities of the spacecraft and its instruments. The first astronauts also had to be small enough to fit into little spacecraft. To date, only about 400 astronauts have travelled into space, but only 26 have ventured further than a low Earth orbit.

FIRST FOR WOMEN

Valentina Tereshkova (1937-) was the first woman in space. She orbited Earth 45 times in Vostok 6, which was launched on 16th June 1963, and Tereshkova returned to Earth by parachute on 19th June. Before she volunteered for space training, Tereshkova was a textile worker who enjoyed parachute jumping as a hobby.

JOHN GLENN

John Glenn, seen here undergoing respiratory testing as part of his training, was the first American to orbit Earth on 20 February 1962. He landed in the Atlantic, after a frightening re-entry in which burning pieces of capsule flew past his window.

FOOD FOR THOUGHT

Astronauts in space need to eat! Food is packed in individual portions and on the Apollo missions, it was freeze-dried, like this pack of beef and vegetables. Hot or cold water was added, and the astronauts then had to suck it out of the packet. Today, the shuttle has an oven. Drinks are taken through special mouthpieces, to stop drops escaping and floating around the spacecraft.

FIRST IN SPACE

Yuri Gagarin (1934-1968), the first man in space, was a pilot in the Soviet Union's Air Force who had volunteered for space training. Gagarin orbited the Earth once on 12 April, 1961, in a Vostock spacecraft. He returned to Earth by ejecting from the spacecraft, and using a parachute to fall the last 4 kilometres (2½ miles) to land. Until this flight, no one knew whether humans would be able to adapt to conditions in space. Overnight, Gagarin became world famous. He was training for a flight in the new Soyuz spacecraft when his MiG-15 aircraft crashed, killing him.

WORKING IN SPACE

To go outside a spacecraft in space, an astronaut must wear a protective suit. Early astronauts were tethered to their craft by a line. Today astronauts use a Manned Manoeuvring Unit (MMU). This is a jet-propelled backpack, like an armchair. Wearing an MMU, an astronaut can travel up to 100 metres (330 feet) from the shuttle. The MMU has enough power for up to 7 hours, enabling an astronaut to work on the outside of a spacecraft or fly to a satellite to bring it across to the shuttle.

THE MERCURY SEVEN

Seven American pilots were chosen for training as the first astronauts. They were (back row from left) Alan Shepard, Virgil 'Gus' Grissom, Gordon Cooper: (front row from left) Walter Schira, Donald 'Deke' Slayton, John Glenn and Scott Carpenter. Americans were shocked when the Soviet Union got a man in space first. Plans to send an American into space were hurriedly brought forward. Alan Shepard, in a Mercury space capsule, landed in the Atlantic after a flight of 15 minutes on 5 May, 1961.

SPACE
-A TIME LINE-

~1925~
Edwin Hubble proves that the Andromeda Nebula is not part of the Milky Way, but a separate galaxy

~1930~
Clyde Tombaugh in America finds the planet Pluto

~1932~
Karl Jansky discovers radio signals coming from space

~1949~
Radio signals discovered to come from stars and other heavenly bodies

~1957~
Sputnik 1, the first satellite, launched by the Soviet Union

~1958~
Explorer 1, America's first satellite, is launched

~1961~
Yuri Gagarin, of the Soviet Union, is the first man in space, on 12 April

Journeys toward the Sun

Humans have only managed to travel a very short distance in space. In order to find out more about the solar system and the bodies in it, space probes are used. A probe is a robot explorer equipped with instruments for measuring, studying, recording, experimenting and photographing. A space probe may take years to reach its destination. It can go past heavenly bodies on its way, taking pictures and gathering information. The first space probes were sent to the Moon and to Venus, the closest planet to Earth. From 1960, the Soviet Union sent a series of 18 Venera probes to the planet. Huge atmospheric pressure and intense heat destroyed many probes, although some of them survived long enough to send back useful information. The American probe Mariner 2 reached Venus in 1962. Between them, the probes collected enormous amounts of information.

CLOUDS ON VENUS

Photographs from space, like this one taken by Mariner 10, show the thick cloudy atmosphere that covers Venus. Although the planet rotates slowly, with a retrograde orbit (it moves in the opposite direction to other planets) the clouds move quickly. They only take four days to circle the planet. They are very dense, and are made up of drops of sulphuric acid and gases such as carbon dioxide.

GIOTTO

Giotto was launched by ESA in 1985, using their Ariane rocket. It encountered Halley's Comet in 1986. It came within 605 kilometres (376 miles) of the core of the comet, showing it to be peanut-shaped, dark and cratered. As well as Giotto, the Soviet Union and Japan sent probes to rendezvous with Halley's comet.

MISSION CONTROL

Every probe is monitored at all times from the ground. Many people work at Mission Control, sending instructions to a spacecraft and working on the information it sends back. Mission Control is an essential part of any operation in space.

SUN SPOTTING

Without our star, the Sun, there would be no life on Earth. From earliest times, people have been interested in the Sun and how it works. Ulysses was built by ESA, and launched from the shuttle Discovery in October 1990. It was designed to orbit the Sun over the Sun's poles. It is examining the solar wind and the particles that make it up.

MAGELLAN PROBE

In 1989, NASA sent the Magellan probe to Venus. Using radar, it has been able to map most of the surface of the planet. The information it collected has allowed scientists to make a 3-D computer model of the surface. They have discovered that Venus is covered in volcanoes.

MERCURY

Mariner 10, the last in a series of American probes, made three fly-bys of Mercury, the planet nearest the Sun. It is the only space probe to have visited Mercury. Launched in 1973, Mariner was protected from the fierce heat of the Sun by a shade and thermal wrappings. Mariner sent back 8,000 photographs that showed Mercury's surface was covered with craters, like the Moon. Mariner 10 also discovered that temperatures on Mercury range from 420°C (800°F) to -180°C (-300°F) and that it has a very thin atmosphere.

Journeys away from the Sun

LOOKING AT MARS

Mariner 9 was launched in 1971, and orbited Mars. It was the first probe to orbit a planet. It took 6,876 photos of the surface. These showed volcanoes, including Olympus Mons, the biggest volcano in the solar system. Mariner found channels like dried-up river beds but it found no sign of vegetation. The probe also took photographs of Mars's two moons, Phobos and Deimos.

Most of the planets in the solar system are further away from the Sun than Earth. Mars, Jupiter and Saturn have been known to astronomers since the earliest times. Uranus was discovered in 1781, Neptune was found in 1846, and Pluto in 1930. An object beyond Pluto was detected in 1992. The farthest reaches of the solar system are largely unexplored. Only Voyager 2 has encountered Neptune. Mars is the second nearest planet to Earth. Over 20 Soviet, American and Japanese probes have been launched to explore it and there are plans for several more. The Pioneer and Voyager probes have, between them, visited Jupiter, Saturn, Uranus and Neptune.

NEXT STOP, SATURN

The Cassini probe to Saturn was launched by NASA in 1997. It is due to arrive in 2004 and will spend four years exploring Saturn, passing all the larger moons in a series of 63 orbits. On board Cassini is an ESA probe named Huyghens, which will be launched into the atmosphere of the moon Titan in 2005. Astronomers think it may be like Earth at the moment when life first appeared. They hope Huyghens may reveal an amazing picture and make many important discoveries.

RINGS AND MOONS

Saturn has been visited by three probes, Pioneer 11 and both Voyagers. They found its rings were made up of millions of tiny chunks of ice, rock and dust. There are hundreds of narrow rings, one kilometre thick. Some are circular, some are oval, and at least one is crooked. Saturn has at least 18 moons! The planet itself has a strong magnetic field, and a very low density.

DISCOVERING NEPTUNE

Voyager 2 was able to visit four planets due to a rare alignment of planets. They were so positioned that on its journey from Earth, Voyager 2 could use the gravity of each planet to push it further into space. Launched in 1977, it took 12 years to reach Neptune. Voyager 2 discovered a huge storm, called the Great Dark Spot. It also discovered six moons, and four very faint rings.

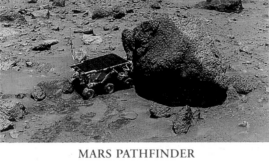

MARS PATHFINDER

The Mars Pathfinder probe sent a craft to the surface of Mars in 1997. The lander released a robot microrover, named Sojourner. Here, Sojourner is analysing a rock nicknamed Yogi. Originally intended to explore Mars for 30 days, Pathfinder kept going three times longer. NASA finally lost touch with Pathfinder in March, 1998.

BY JUPITER!

Pioneer 10 was launched in March 1972 and encountered Jupiter in December 1973. It was the first probe to travel beyond Mars, and the first to navigate the asteroid belt. Pioneer 10 took the first close-up pictures of Jupiter. It could not find any solid surface on the planet, and also discovered that Jupiter has a magnetic field 2,000 times stronger than Earth's.

SPACE
-A Time Line-

~1961~
Alan Shepard is the first American in space, on 5 May

25th May: President Kennedy challenges America to put a man on the Moon within 10 years

~1962~
Telstar, the world's first commercial satellite, is launched

~1963~
Arecibo radio telescope built

~1969~
Apollo 11 is launched on its journey to the Moon, 16 July

Neil Armstrong is the first man on the Moon, 20 July

~1975~
Very Large Array first used

~1977~
Voyagers 1 and 2 launched

~1980~
Voyager 1 encounters Saturn, then leaves solar system

~1981~
First space shuttle flight (shuttle Columbia)

~1986~
Giotto encounters Halley's Comet

Challenger disaster: space shuttle blows up 73 seconds after launch

First part of space station Mir placed in orbit

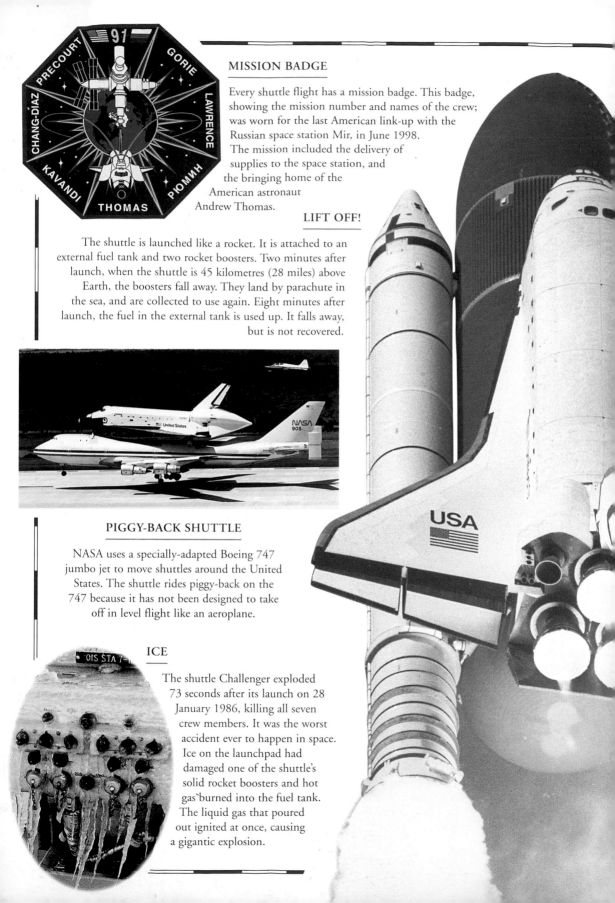

MISSION BADGE

Every shuttle flight has a mission badge. This badge, showing the mission number and names of the crew; was worn for the last American link-up with the Russian space station Mir, in June 1998. The mission included the delivery of supplies to the space station, and the bringing home of the American astronaut Andrew Thomas.

LIFT OFF!

The shuttle is launched like a rocket. It is attached to an external fuel tank and two rocket boosters. Two minutes after launch, when the shuttle is 45 kilometres (28 miles) above Earth, the boosters fall away. They land by parachute in the sea, and are collected to use again. Eight minutes after launch, the fuel in the external tank is used up. It falls away, but is not recovered.

PIGGY-BACK SHUTTLE

NASA uses a specially-adapted Boeing 747 jumbo jet to move shuttles around the United States. The shuttle rides piggy-back on the 747 because it has not been designed to take off in level flight like an aeroplane.

ICE

The shuttle Challenger exploded 73 seconds after its launch on 28 January 1986, killing all seven crew members. It was the worst accident ever to happen in space. Ice on the launchpad had damaged one of the shuttle's solid rocket boosters and hot gas burned into the fuel tank. The liquid gas that poured out ignited at once, causing a gigantic explosion.

The Space Shuttle

Sending probes and satellites into space using rockets is extremely expensive. To reduce the cost, the Americans designed a reusable space craft – the shuttle. There are four shuttles, each launched regularly throughout the year. The shuttle is used to launch, retrieve and repair satellites. It is also used as a laboratory during the 14 days it can stay in orbit. Each shuttle mission has a commander, a pilot and a number of other specialists some of whom perform spacewalks and undertake scientific experiments on board.

SWEET DREAMS

In space there is no down or up, so astronauts can sleep anywhere. Sally Ride, the first female American astronaut, is seen here in a sleeping bag attached to the sides of the craft. This prevents her floating around. She knows she'll wake up in the same place!

IN CONTROL

All the controls for the space shuttle are located in the cockpit. There are controls for flying the shuttle, controls for all the systems in the shuttle such as air and power, and controls for external operations and the cargo in the payload bay. The commander sits in the left-hand seat in the cockpit, looking forward, and the pilot sits in the right-hand seat.

SMOOTH LANDINGS

When it is ready to return to Earth after a mission, the shuttle uses its engines to brake. As it slows, it falls towards Earth. As it falls through the atmosphere, the shuttle heats up, and the air around it glows. The hot air stops the radios working for about 10 minutes. The crew is protected from the heat by the shuttle's coat of ceramic tiles.

Nearer the ground, the shuttle uses wing and tail flaps and a parachute to slow it down further. Then it lands like a glider.

Telescopes Today

Professional astronomers
rarely look through
telescopes! Most of
their work is done
on computers. This
astronomer works on
images received by signals
from a radio telescope.

The observatory, at
Plateau de Bure in France,
has five dishes, and
explores pulsars - stars
which are the source of
very regular radio signals -
in distant galaxies.

A great deal of astronomical exploration and fact-finding is still done with Earth-based telescopes. Satellites have provided a wealth of information, but most of them are looking at one object, such as the Sun, or are only working in a particular area of radiation, such as X-rays. Astronomers today use optical telescopes housed in observatories built in high, dry places where there is a clear atmosphere, and no light pollution. Most optical telescopes are big reflectors, attached to cameras and controlled by computers. Radio waves coming from bodies in space were first noticed in 1932, but radio telescopes were not developed until after World War II. Radio telescopes listen, rather than look. They collect weaker signals than optical telescopes, so can explore much further out in space. Radio telescopes have found radio sources such as pulsars and quasars in the heavens, and detected objects 13,000,000,000 light years away from Earth.

BIG BANG

Satellite telescopes have opened up a vast new range of space for astronomers to explore. One question they are keen to answer is how the universe began. The Big Bang theory proposes that it started with a gigantic explosion about 15,000,000,000 years ago. COBE, the Cosmic Background Explorer, was launched in 1989 to study the microwave radiation that can be found very faintly everywhere in the universe. COBE discovered that it rippled, as it would do if it were the remains of the Big Bang.

THE VERY LARGE ARRAY

A radio telescope has an antenna in a dish. Radio waves from space, sent from a natural body like a star or from a man-made spacecraft, are bounced off the dish, collected by the antenna, and converted into electronic signals that can be 'read' by a computer. Several radio telescopes can be used together like one large one. This allows astronomers to collect signals from far away in space, and to get more detailed images than they can get from optical telescopes. The Very Large Array, in New Mexico, America, has 27 movable dishes, each with a diameter of 25 metres.

MAUNA KEA

Many countries, including America, Britain, Canada, France and Hawaii have optical telescopes at observatories on the Mauna Kea volcano in Hawaii. At a height of 14,000 feet, they are above a third of Earth's atmosphere. As well as giving clearer pictures, the observatories stay cool. It is important that the instruments are not affected by temperature changes as this distorts the image.

SOHO

SOHO - the Solar Heliospheric Observatory - is a satellite launched by ESA which orbits the Sun. It has 12 instruments that study the solar atmosphere and how the Sun is made up. An ultraviolet camera photographs the Sun at four different temperatures each day. SOHO's photographs have recorded activity such as massive explosions and a sunquake with seismic waves two miles high travelling at 250,000 miles an hour.

284 angstroms

195 angstroms

171 angstroms

304 angstroms

AMATEUR ASTRONOMY

Many amateur astronomers enjoy watching the heavens and heavenly bodies as a hobby. Some collect information that is useful to professional astronomers. Many comets have been found and have had their orbits constantly monitored by amateur astronomers.

SPACE
-A Time Line-

~1989~
Voyager 2 encounters Neptune, then leaves solar system

~1990~
Hubble Space Telescope launched

~1993~
Hubble Space Telescope repaired on space shuttle

~1995~
Galileo probe visits Jupiter

~1997~
Mars Pathfinder sends a lander, including robot microrover Sojourner, to the surface of Mars

Cassini/Huyghens probe launched. Cassini due to encounter Saturn in 2004, Huyghens due to descend into Titan's atmosphere in 2005

~1998~
Russians announce that space station Mir will be decommissioned in 1999.

23

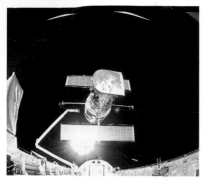

HUBBLE TELESCOPE

When the Hubble Space Telescope was launched, scientists were horrified to find that the images it sent back to Earth were blurred. They discovered that its 96 inch (2.4 metre) main mirror had been ground to the wrong shape. Although it was less than a hair's width wrong, it was enough to cause NASA great embarrassment.

The Hubble Space Telescope

The Hubble Space Telescope is a satellite built by NASA and ESA and launched in 1990. It is a reflecting telescope, and also works in ultraviolet. The satellite receives power from two solar panels. The volume of space Hubble can cover is 350 times bigger than can be seen from Earth. It is designed to look a long way beyond the solar system and collect information about how stars and galaxies evolve. The Hubble Space Telescope was designed to be repaired as necessary by shuttle astronauts. So far, two repair missions have taken place and it is still going strong.

EDWIN HUBBLE

Edwin Hubble (1889-1953), after whom the Hubble Space Telescope was named, was an American astronomer who was interested in nebulae and galaxies. He proved that our Galaxy, the Milky Way, was not the only galaxy.

HUBBLE OPTICS

Satellites are built in sterile, temperature-controlled atmospheres, as dust or temperature changes could ruin the working of delicate instruments. Grinding mirrors and making lenses for telescopes requires great accuracy. The making of the optical parts of the Hubble Space Telescope was carried out with extreme care.

TO THE RESCUE

The space shuttle Endeavour was launched in 1993 on a mission to repair the telescope. Two astronauts caught the telescope and hauled it into the shuttle's payload bay, using the robot Remote Manipulator Arm. The solar panels were replaced. The Wide Field Planetary Camera was replaced and the faulty lens was corrected. Other instruments were checked or updated. The repairs took 35 hours of spacewalks, and were completely successful.

BEFORE AND AFTER

These two pictures show how much improvement there was to photographs after the Hubble Space Telescope was repaired. On the left is a photograph of the M100 galaxy taken with the faulty lens. On the right is the same galaxy taken with the repaired lens. Astronomers can now see star clusters and individual stars.
M100 is tens of millions of light years away. It is found in the constellation Virgo.

MIR

Space station Mir is built of several sections, or modules. Each has a different purpose. The core module contains the main living cabin with others containing laboratories and docking ports. Solar panels stick out in all directions. Space shuttle Atlantis uses a special docking adapter to join the space station.

IN A SPIN

An American schoolchild suggested an experiment to see if spiders could spin webs in space. Spiders Anita and Arabella flew on Skylab. Being in free fall confused Arabella and she could not spin a web properly for the first two days. Anita was not allowed to spin for several days. She could make good webs at once when she was allowed to start.

RENDEZVOUS

1995 saw the start of a two-year programme in which America and Russia worked together in space. Russian cosmonauts flew in the shuttle Atlantis, and American astronauts worked on space station Mir. At their first meeting, the two crews posed in the spacelab module in Atlantis's payload bay for this group photograph. Mir commander Vladimir Dezhurov is on the left, behind the man with crossed arms. Atlantis commander Robert 'Hoot' Gibson is upside down, top right – about one o'clock.

Space Stations

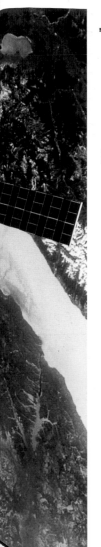

A space station is an enormous satellite. It is so big that astronauts can live and work in it for much longer than they could on a spacecraft. To date, there have been eight Soviet space stations: seven called Salyut and the current Russian one, Mir. America has had one space station, Skylab, and ESA built one called Spacelab, which is used in the space shuttle's payload bay. On a space station, longer and more complicated experiments can be carried out than on other craft. This is very important for future space exploration. Valuable information can be gathered on how humans cope with long spells of weightlessness. Astronauts from many countries have also worked on such things as making drugs in very pure forms to help sick people on Earth.

DOOR TO DOOR DELIVERY

Astronauts look out of the windows as Atlantis arrives at Mir to deliver supplies. This mission included delivery of a docking module. Docking the space shuttle with space station Mir took careful manoeuvring, as Mir orbits Earth at a speed of 27,000 kilometres (17,000 miles) an hour.

WEIGHTLESSNESS

Being in free fall, or weightless, in space looks fun, as Skylab astronauts Edward Gibson (floating) and Gerald Carr demonstrate! But it produces medical problems. Astronauts who live on space stations have to exercise for up to three hours every day to try and keep fit. They also take extra vitamins and calcium. Soviet cosmonauts have worked on Mir for over a year, but no one yet knows what would happen to someone travelling in space for a very long time.

KEEPING CLEAN

Astronauts on board Skylab used a shower which pulled up and sealed round the astronaut's body. Water was air-blasted through a hand-held shower head and then vacuumed off - a bit like drying yourself with a hoover! The shower leaked. So now, on the shuttle, astronauts have sponge baths, using a wash basin.

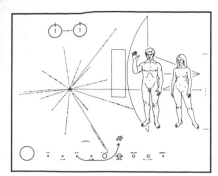

Making Contact

Two Pioneer space probes, numbers 10 and 11, had an extra mission. After their work exploring the asteroids, Jupiter and Saturn, they headed for deep space. Each probe has an identical plaque on the outside, engraved with symbols. They show a hydrogen atom, the sun giving off radio energy, a diagram of the solar system showing which planet Pioneer came from, and a male and female figure in front of an outline of Pioneer to the same scale.

*T*here are millions of stars in millions of galaxies. Scientists believe there must be many planets orbiting the stars. They hope that life may have evolved on some of them. It is possible that some of that life might be intelligent. Earth has sent messages into space, hoping to make contact. Space is vast and we have only developed the technology to get in touch in the last thirty or forty years. Attempts have also been made to see if anyone has tried to get in touch with us. Since the early days of radio astronomy, scientists have been interested in finding radio signals that have been sent out deliberately. In 1992, NASA started a 10-year programme, SETI (Search for Extra Terrestrial Intelligence). Nearby stars were to be searched, and the entire sky scanned for microwaves. Radio telescopes around the world are studying the nearest 1,000 stars. So far, no contact has been made in either direction.

CROP CIRCLES

Have intelligent beings from space ever visited Earth? Some people think they have. Crop circles, and other geometric shapes, appear from time to time in fields of grain and other plants. They are particularly found on the chalk downlands of Salisbury Plain in southern England. There is usually no obvious path connecting them with a human access point. One theory about them is that they are made by beings from space who want to communicate with us. Other theories include local climatic disturbances, herds of madly rotating hedgehogs, and ordinary vandals!

LONG DISTANCE MESSAGE

The radio telescope at Arecibo is the world's biggest. It is built into a hollow in the hills of Puerto Rico, and uses the Earth's rotation to sweep the skies. In 1974, astronomers sent a message from Arecibo out into space. The message took three minutes to send, and was directed towards the M13 galaxy in the constellation Hercules. It will take 25,000 years to travel to M13!

CLOSE ENCOUNTERS

The idea that Earth has been visited by beings from space has inspired many films. Steven Spielberg gave some of the profits he made from the film ET to the SETI Institute for research. It funded META, the Megachannel Extra Terrestrial Assay, which used the 26 metre telescope at Harvard University in Massachusetts for a major search of the northern skies.

GOLD DISCS

The probes Voyager 1 and 2 explored Jupiter, Saturn, Uranus and Neptune, then left the solar system and headed for deep space. Each carries an identical gold-plated LP record, the 'Sounds of Earth'. On the record are greetings in 60 languages, animal sounds, natural noises like thunder, the sea and the wind, music and pictures of life on Earth. There are also instructions on how to play the records.

DESERT PICTURES

In the deserts of southern Peru there are giant images of animals such as a spider, a bird and a monkey. These Nazca lines are over 1,000 years old and some are miles long. They are made by piling up the dark surface stones to show the paler stones beneath. They can only be seen properly from the air, but were made long before any known flight.

The Future

The future for the exploration of space looks very exciting. Many more satellites are planned. Probes will range out as far as Pluto and the Kuyper Belt, and land on a comet and an asteroid. A new international space station is being built and it's expected that humans will walk again on the Moon shortly after the start of the third millennium. Living on a Moon base would probably come soon after. An astronaut on Mars may not be too far away.

TO BOLDLY GO...

The imagination of writers and artists has always outrun the abilities of scientists and engineers. Travelling to the stars is a long way off in reality. It is hard enough to explore the solar system. We have no way of travelling faster than light, which we would have to do to reach the stars. But with imaginative creations like Starship Enterprise we can roam the galaxies.

MOON BASE

In 1998, water ice was discovered at the poles of the Moon. Water on the Moon makes establishing a Moon base a much easier proposition. Ice could be melted into water and used for drinking, washing, and growing plants. It could be turned into oxygen to breathe, and hydrogen to use as fuel.

DELTA CLIPPER

One priority for the future is a new space transport system. The Delta Clipper is being tested as one possible successor to the Shuttle. It takes off and lands vertically. Powered by eight rocket engines, it moves from Earth to orbit in only one stage, and can carry loads up to 10 tonnes (20,000 lbs) weight. It can be used with or without a crew. Farther into the future, rockets that use nuclear fuel may become possible. They could be used for very long missions.

A SPACE LOO

'How do you go to the lavatory?' is a question astronauts are often asked. There have been lavatories in space since space station Skylab, which was operational in 1973-4.

The astronaut wears rubber gloves, and uses handles and foot rests to hold him- or herself on the seat. Air is used to suck wastes down a funnel into a disposable container. Solid waste is dried and compacted. Wet wipes are used for cleaning both the astronaut and the lavatory. This 'waste management compartment' was designed by NASA to use on the new space station.

INTERNATIONAL SPACE STATION

In 1998, Russia announced it was going to decommission the Mir space station in 1999, after 13 years' service. A new space station has been under discussion for about 10 years. It would be international, with each of 16 countries in the project building different parts. Building the International Space Station should take six years, from 1998 to 2004. Space shuttles will fly engineers, components and other supplies to the station.

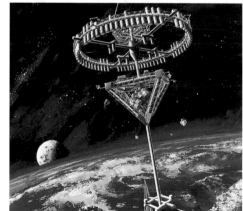

SPACE HOTEL

Spend your holidays in space! The idea of an orbiting hotel has been under investigation by several Japanese companies for some years. The whole complex would be inside, safely sealed away from the freezing vacuum of space.

STATION LIFE

Early space stations look very cluttered, with boxes and equipment everywhere. The new station will be designed to have tidy working areas and living quarters. Astronauts will each have a cubicle, with storage space, a worktable, computer terminal and a sleeping bag.

DID YOU KNOW?

Why many amateur astronomers like to watch for comets? A comet is named for the person who first reports it – it could be you!

Why the first American astronauts had to be less than 1.8 metres (5ft 11ins) high? Taller men would not be able to fit into the tiny spacecraft! Astronauts also had to be under 40, physically fit, have a university degree or the equivalent, and be a test pilot with at least 1,500 hours of flying time. The Soviet Union's cosmonauts were even shorter. They had to be under 1.7 metres (5ft 7ins) tall. They also had to be pilots, fit, and under 30.

What the word 'astronaut' means? It's Latin for 'sailor in the stars'.

What a shuttle launch costs? More than half a billion dollars! It also takes the work of 40,000 engineers and space scientists.

How fast humans are launched into space by rocket travel? It's 11 kilometres (7 miles) a second. As they wait to be launched, they are sitting on the equivalent of a firework 30 metres (100 feet) high.

What a huge number of parts there are in a rocket or spacecraft? America's first spacecraft, the Mercury, contained 11 kilometres (7 miles) of electric wire. There were 30,000 parts in a Saturn 5 rocket.

How for centuries people have dreamed about journeying to the Moon? Around 165 AD, the writer Lucian of Samosata wrote the first known space story. His *Vera Historia*, or True History, relates the adventures of a shipload of Greek athletes who are blown to the Moon.

How great the atmospheric pressure at the surface of Venus is? It's 90 times greater than that of Earth. It is so hot that lead would melt.

How much fuel the space shuttle uses? More than 680,000 kilos of liquid oxygen and hydrogen. The shuttle's three engines only work for 8 minutes on each flight. In that time, they use all the fuel – and the shuttle has travelled from Earth into space.

ACKNOWLEDGEMENTS

The publishers would like to thank: Graham Rich and Hazel Poole for their assistance.
Copyright © 1998 ticktock Publishing Ltd.
First published in Great Britain by ticktock Publishing Ltd, The Offices in the Square, Hadlow, Tonbridge, Kent, TN11 0DD. All rights reserved.
No part of this publication may be reproduced, stored in a retrieval system, or transmitted in any form or by any means electronic, mechanical, photocopying, recording or otherwise, without prior written permission of the copyright owner.

A CIP catalogue record for this book is available from the British Library. ISBN 1 86007 079 5
Picture research by Image Select. Printed in Great Britain.

Picture Credits: t=top, b=bottom, c=centre, l=left, r=right, OFC=outside front cover, OBC=outside back cover, IFC=inside front cover

Ann Ronan; 6cl. Ann Ronan @ Image Select; 2cl, 3br, 4tl, 5br, 5tr, 6/7t & OBC, 7cl, 8ct, 8cr, 13tl, 15ct & OFC. Bridgemann Art Library; 2cb, 2/3cb, 4bl, 5tl, 6/7b, 6tl, 7br. British Museum; 5c. Fratelli Alinari; 6b. Images; 29bl. Image Select; 2/3c, 7cr. Kobal Collection; 28/29c & OFC, 30tl & OBC. National Maritime Museum; 4/5c & OFC. NASA; 15br & OBC, 31t. Novosti (London); 10bl, 11bl. Planet Earth Pictures; 8l & OFC, 8/9b, 9tr, 10tl, 11ct, 12cl, 13br, 14/15b, 16tl, 16/17c, 17cb, 17ct, 18/19c, 19c, 19bl, 20cl, 20bl, 20tl, 21tr, 22/23c, 23cr, 25t, 26tl, 27bl, 26/27b, 28tl. Rex Features; 14tl, 26bl. Science Photo Library; 12bl, 12/13b, (George Baird/US Army) 30/31b, (John Bova) 23cb, (Julian Baum) 16bl, 16/17(main pic), (John Fassanito/NASA) 26/27t, (Bruce Frisch) 31cb, (Philippe Gontier/Eurelios) 22tl, (Hale Observatories) 24/25b, (Galia Jerrican) 22bl, (NASA) 8/9b, 10cb, 11br, 12tr, 14br, 27tr, 29c, 30cb, (Novosti) 8cb, 10/11c, 12/13b & OFC, (David Parker) 28bl, 29tr, (Space Telescope Science Institute/NASA) 25bl & 25br, (Deltev van Ravenswaay) 23t & IFC. Shimizu Corporation; 31br. Telegraph Colour Library; 2tl, 3ct & OFC, 12cr & OBC, 12tl & OFC, 14/15t & 32c & OFC, 18tl, 19t, 20/21c, 21br, 21c, 24tl, 24bl

Every effort has been made to trace the copyright holders and we apologize in advance for any unintentional omissions.
We would be pleased to insert the appropriate acknowledgement in any subsequent edition of this publication.